Peter the Pelican

If You Want a Friend, You Must Be a Friend

D1002537

Written By:

Jerry "Pop" Bishop
and
Dr. Gail Bishop Dugger

Illustrated by:

H. Steven Robertson

PUBLISHED BY HIGH PITCHED HUM PUBLISHING
321 15th Street North
Jacksonville Beach, Florida 32250

www.highpitchedhum.net
www.jettyman.com

HIGH PITCHED HUM and the mosquito are trademarks of High Pitched Hum Publishing.

The cataloging-in-publication data is on file with the Library of Congress.

ISBN: 978-1-934666-23-4 Copyright © 2008 by Jerry Bishop

Copyright © 2008 art by H. Steven Robertson

Printed in the United States of America

May, 2008

This book is dedicated in honor of my sister,

Nadine Reddick

(Pictured: Nadine with Husband, Hulon Reddick)

Nadine's positive influence on my life and her great love for me, her baby brother, has been a blessing. She has been my counselor and my advisor all of my life. I will always be grateful and indebted to her for the many things she has done for my family and me. I love you, too, Naney.

Your brother Jerry

a note from the illustrator

This new Peter the Pelican book is done with the same meticulous attention to detail as the first. Every creature was researched and/or studied and each drawing came from real-life examples. All of the poses and color variations are authentic. Like Pop, I am a sportsman, an avid fisherman and lover of wildlife. We both inhabit and fish the southern coastal areas of the eastern seaboard on the Atlantic Ocean.

As any experienced fisherman will tell you, you have but to clean your fish on any dock near the ocean and you will attract flocks of birds—almost all pelicans, seagulls and egrets. They all seek the fisherman's friendship, hoping and begging for free handouts. They have lost most of their fear of man and get pretty close, sometimes too close. And, it is common for a pod of playful dolphins to be rolling and cavorting in the water nearby.

Again like Pop, I am an avid nature lover and it is difficult to take my eyes off of these creatures. Indeed, some of the photos used as examples were taken on the Pilot station dock in Mayport, Florida, while I was cleaning fish. I love the pelicans. They are a big, sweet bird and sometimes they even wag their tails. It is easy to see how Pop enjoys the friendship of Peter.

H. Steven Robertson
Illustrator

In loving memory of

Linsey Rae Bishop

1990 · 2006

And love to the rest of the gang

Branyon Michael "Digger" Dugger

Kyler Chastain Bishop

Bryan Thomas Miller

Wyatt Lee Dugger

Hello, my name is Peter "the fisheater" Pelican.
My friend's name is Pop.

ROBERTSON
3 2008

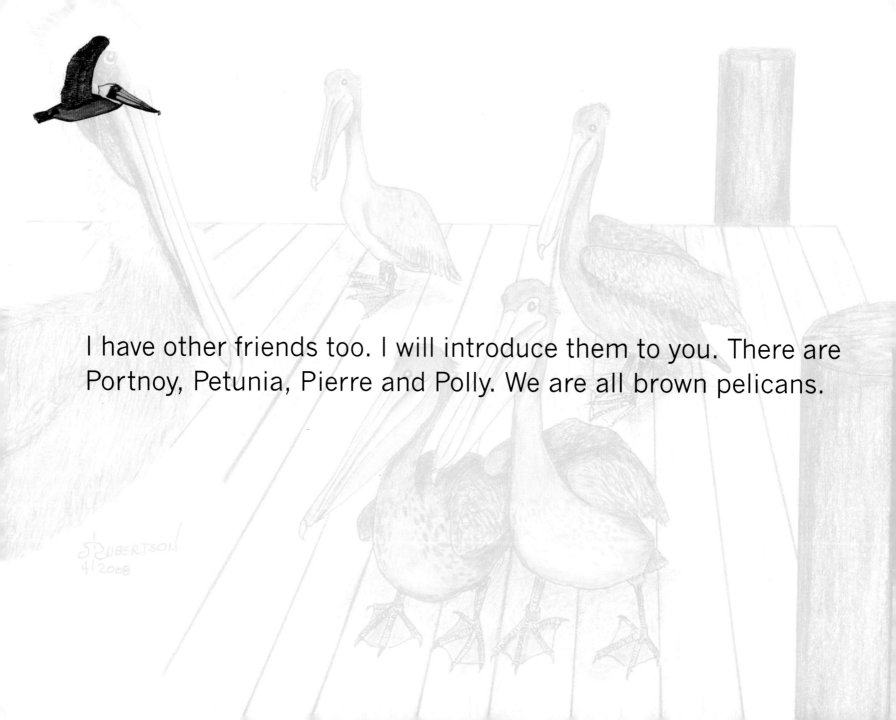

I have other friends too. I will introduce them to you. There are Portnoy, Petunia, Pierre and Polly. We are all brown pelicans.

We also have friends that are different from us. There is Gilly Gull. Pop calls him "Silly Gilly" because he is always making funny loud noises. Next is Ed Egret. Ed Egret is a Great Egret. Pop nicknamed him "Sticks" because he has long skinny black legs that look like tree limbs.

Then there is Danny Dolphin. He is a very fast swimmer and does amusing tricks by jumping out of the water, spinning and doing somersaults in the air. We all get along really well because we respect each other and help each other.

S. ROBERTSON
4' 2008

I remember one time when Pop told us he was going to be gone for several days and he wouldn't be here to feed us. Well, the day he left the wind began to blow really hard. The waves got big and the water got murky. We were unable to fly and dive so we couldn't find any fish to eat. We were getting really hungry.

Then Danny Dolphin appeared nodding his head and swimming backwards.

Petunia said, "I think he wants us to follow him." So we jumped off the dock, into the water and started swimming with our webbed feet.

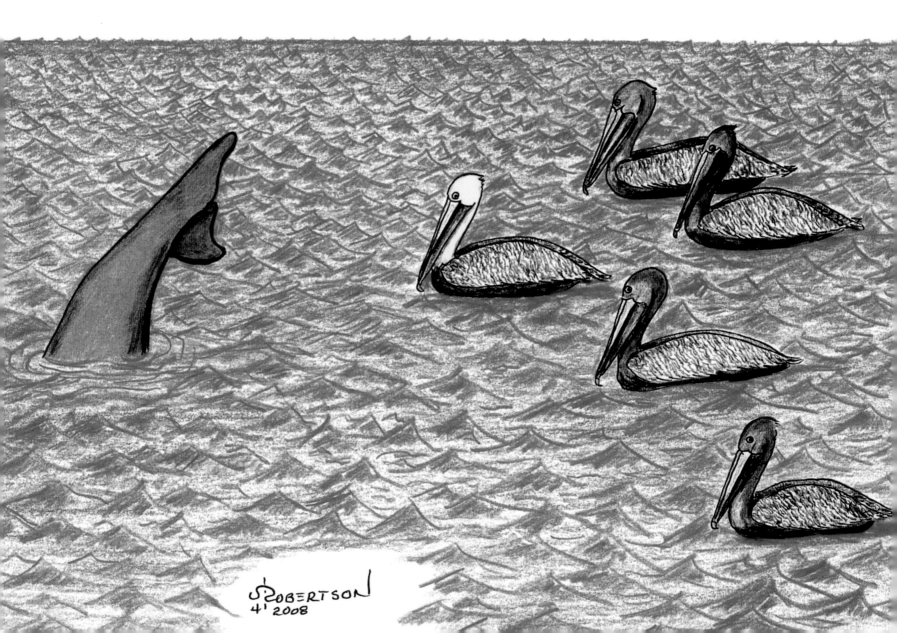

We followed Danny and then he disappeared going down deep in the water. All at once a big school of small mullet fish came to the surface with Danny right below them.

S ROBERTSON
4 2008

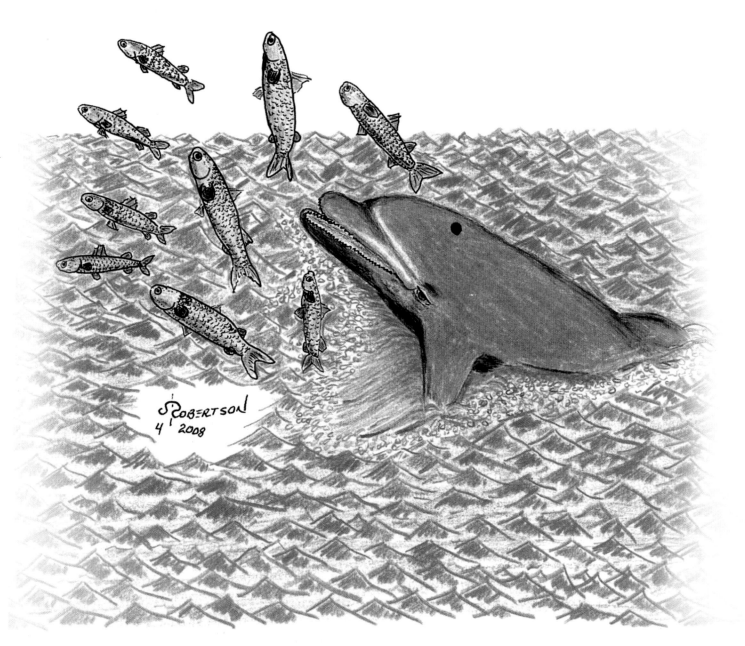

We started grabbing them with our long beaks. Danny started knocking them high in the sky. We would catch them in the air. That was really fun. We finally got full and swam back to the dock. Our friend Danny Dolphin had led us to food.

When Pop returned from his trip, his neighbor came over to tell him about Danny feeding us. He and Pop talked about friendship.

Pop said that friends help each other. He told us that friends are reliable, dependable and always ready to help.

SROBERTSON
4/2008

Pop said that even when friends disagree they don't get mad or say hurtful things. Also, we must choose our friends very carefully because not everyone wants to be our friend. I heard Pop tell his neighbor that when he was a young boy his big sister, Nadine told him, "If you want a friend, you must be a friend".

ROBERTSON
4 | 2008

We all agree that if you want a friend, you must be a friend and we have made it our motto. If you agree then join us.

Ready? One, two, three. "If you want a friend, be a friend!

The End.

Fun Animal Facts

LAUGHING GULLS

⚓ The Laughing Gull makes a loud noise that sounds like "ha-ha-ha."

⚓ They live around beaches, fresh water, and also in parking lots and garbage dumpsters.

⚓ The bird is normally diurnal, but during the breeding season, forages at night as well.

⚓ The male and female Laughing Gull usually build their nest together.

⚓ The gulls lay three to four greenish eggs in a grass nest and the babies hatch in about three weeks.

⚓ The adult Laughing Gull removes the eggshells from the nest after the eggs hatch.

⚓ As an adult, the head is black and its bill is dark red. In the winter, they have a mottled gray head and a black bill.

⚓ The Laughing Gull is a wonderful flier and good swimmer, although it seldom dives underwater.

⚓ The gulls are famous for begging around people who are picnicking or fishing.

GREAT WHITE EGRETS

⚓ The Great White egret flies with its neck retracted in an s-shape.

⚓ To feed, they wade in shallow water and spear fish, frogs, ells, and crabs with their long, sharp bill.

⚓ Egrets are very patient and can stand totally still for a long time when hunting their food.

⚓ The Great Egret can be distinguished from other egrets by its yellow bill and black legs and feet.

⚓ In Florida, the Great Egret is sometimes confused with the Great White Heron.

⚓ In Florida and other places, the Great Egret used to be hunted and their plumes (feathers) were sold to decorate hats.

⚓ The species was chosen as a symbol of the National Audubon Society, which was formed in part to prevent the killing of the bird for their feathers.

⚓ As a result of conservation measures, the numbers of birds have increased since the 19th century.

BROWN PELICANS

⚓ Brown pelicans are the smallest of all pelicans.

⚓ The pouch beneath the beak of the brown pelican can hold two to three times as much as the bird's stomach.

⚓ To swallow a fish, the brown pelican must stick its beak straight up.

⚓ The brown pelicans stay close to salt water like the ocean or rivers that empty into the ocean.
⚓ They are rarely seen more than 20 miles from land.

⚓ Nests are built on the ground or in low trees by both the male and female brown pelican.

⚓ The female brown pelican lays two to three eggs that hatch in about one month.

⚓ The brown pelican stands of its eggs with its web feet until they hatch.

⚓ Parents of the brown pelicans catch fish, grind them up, then take it to the nest and spit it up so the babies can eat.

⚓ Brown pelicans sometimes fly in a v-shaped formation. They love riding on "thermals" which is warm air that rises above water or structures on land.

DOLPHINS

⚓ Dolphins are related to whales and porpoises.

⚓ The limbs on the front of their body are called flippers and their tail is called a fluke.

⚓ They are mammals and give live birth to their young.

⚓ The dolphin is considered to be among the most intelligent of animals.

⚓ Their often friendly attitude and appearance makes them popular with humans.

⚓ They normally swim about 3-7 miles per hour with bursts up to 20 mph.

⚓ Unlike most mammals they have no hair.

⚓ They have acute eyesight both in and out of water.

⚓ Their hearing is much better than humans.

⚓ They must be conscious to breathe so they cannot go into a deep sleep because they would suffocate.

⚓ They have solved this problem by letting one half their brain sleep at a time.

⚓ They sleep about 8 hours a day in this fashion.

⚓ On average they eat anywhere from 22 to 50 pounds of fish a day.

⚓ The maximum life is 40 to 50 years.

⚓ The average life expectancy is about 25 years but even this depends on where they live.

⚓ They do not drink salt water. They get their water from the fish they eat.

⚓ There are about 30-40 different species of dolphins.

J ROBERTSON
4 ' 2008

Tips on Friendship

We all need friends because it is not good to be alone. A friend is somebody that knows all about you and still loves you. A friend is one who never gets in the way unless you are going the wrong way. Friends provide strength and encouragement.

A poet once wrote, "I went out to find a friend but could not find one there.
I went out to be a friend and found friends everywhere".

Ways you can be a good friend...

- Make your friends feel they are special.

- Compliment your friends, don't say ugly things, say good things.

- Be loyal and true to your friends.

- Treat your friends the way you want to be treated.

- Keep secrets that a friend tells you.

- Pay attention when your friend is talking.

- Keep your promises.

- Share things with your friends.

- Tell your friend the truth, don't lie.

- Stand up for your friends.

- If your parents discourage you from having certain friends,
  listen to them. They would not deny you a friend without good reason.

It is okay to agree to disagree with a friend, but do it in a nice way.

Questions for Readers

1. What is Peter's nickname?

2. What is Gilly Gull's nickname?

3. What is Ed Egret's nickname?

4. What did Danny do to get Peter and his friends to follow him?

5. How many pelican friends does Peter have and what are their names?

6. Does Peter have any other friends?

7. Why do they all get along?

8. Why couldn't Peter and his pelican friends fly and dive for fish?

9. Which one of their friends came to help them when they were hungry?

10. How did he help them?

11. What kind of fish did Danny find?

12. Why did Peter and his friends think they were having fun while eating?

13. How did Pop find out about Danny feeding Peter and his friends?

14. What advice did Pop's sister, Nadine, give him?

Write a story about you and one of your friends.

_____

_____

_____

_____

_____

_____

_____

_____

_____

_____

_____

_____

_____

_____

_____

_____

_____

_____

About the Authors

Jerry "Pop" Bishop is a retired educator. He spent 37 years as a teacher, coach, and administrator. His master's degree is from Arkansas State University in school administration. Pop Bishop has had an avid interest in fish and wildlife since he was big enough to hold a fishing pole. He now resides on a tidal river in Georgia where the fish and wildlife are abundant. Although his writing is basically fictional much of it is also true.

Dr. Gail Bishop Dugger is the Assistant Principal of St. Marys Elementary School in St. Marys, Georgia. Dr. Dugger has been an educator for 30 years, 25 of those years as a classroom teacher. She received her BSE and MS from Arkansas State University in Elementary and Special Education. She received her Doctoral degree from Nova Southeastern University in Educational Leadership. She resides in Callahan, Florida with her husband Mike. Gail is an avid reader, loves to watch movies, enjoys shopping, and is especially fond of spending time with her family.

The authors can be reached at: peterthepelican@aol.com or www.pelicanenterprises.com

About the Illustrator

H. Steven Robertson was born and raised in Florida. He lives with his wife Kathy, daughters, Summer and Sunny, and son-in-law, Taylor, in Neptune Beach, Florida. Steve graduated from Newberry College in South Carolina in 1967 and received his master's degree from the University of Florida in 1972. For 37 years, Mr. Robertson worked in various jobs as a public school educator including teaching, dean of boys, administrative assistant, and librarian. He also coached football, soccer, softball, track, swimming and most other sports. He retired as an assistant principal in 2004.

In addition to Peter the Pelican, Mr. Robertson has done the cover art and illustrations for many published novels. He is the author of Ranch Boy, Bottom Time, The Stream, Acorns of Love and Wisdom, Soccer Made Easy For Americans, and An Exercise Manual For the Couch Potato. *Steve can be reached at: coachrtoo@yahoo.com or www.ranchboybooks.com*